Short Walks in the Keswick and Borrowdale Area

The Lake District National Park

The Lake District National park is the biggest of England's national Parks. Its 885 square mile mile area is best loved for the variety and contrast of its landscape. Here you can see high fells, rocky crags, lush green dales with long still lakes, vibrant villages and quiet hamlets. You can also see England's highest mountain (Scafell Pike) and her deepest lake (Wastwater), as well as investigating the history of literary legends such as Wordsworth.

The Lake District National Park is a celebration of how people and nature can work together. Although the Lake District countryside may seem wild, it looks the way it does because of human activity, particularly farming. People have been using the area for at least 10,000 years and in 1951 it was established as a National Park to protect it for future generations.

The land of the Lake District National Park is nearly all privately owned and much of it farmed. Because of this it is especially important that you use the Country Code to guide your activities in the National Park.

Short Walks in the Keswick and Borrowdale Area

Paul Buttle

Published by
amadorn

I would like to express here my thanks to Hilary
Drummond and Pat Clark for the help they have
given me producing this guide.

ISBN 0 9519345 6 2
First published in the second quarter of the penultimate year of the second
millennium and reprinted in the third quarter of the year prior to the third
millennium.

Published by Amadorn, 18 Brewery Lane, Keswick, Cumbria.
Typeset in Palatino by An Údar, 18 Greta Villas, Keswick, Cumbria.
Printed by Nuffield Press, Abingdon, Oxfordshire

Contents

Introduction   6

1   Castlehead   8

2   Newlands Valley   10

3   Seatoller to Seathwaite   12

4   The River Derwent   14

5   Friar's Crag and Calfclose Bay   16

6   Cat Bells Terrace and the   18
    Brandelhow Shoreline

7   Dean's Trod to Ashness Bridge   20

8   Surprise View   22

9   Borrowdale Terrace   24

10 Stonethwaite Valley   26

11 Castlerigg Stone Circle   28

12 The Watendlath Valley   30

13 Dock Tarn   32

14 Walla Crag   34

Public Transport   36

Introduction

What is a short walk and what is a long walk is a matter of opinion. But few, I'm sure, will think the walks described in this book are other than short, except possibly for the Walla Crag walk and the Dock Tarn walk. They are all on the whole fairly easy rambles which bring great rewards for the effort involved.

Suggested times and how the walks are ordered.

Each walk has a suggested time but this should be regarded simply as a rule of thumb. I've tended to give, I think, a fairly generous time allowances but some users may not think so. I have not allowed for stops, so if you are a person who likes plenty of stops allow yourself more time. The walks are ordered, roughly, according to the effort involved in completing them. Thus the easiest walk is first and the hardest last.

What map to use?

When going on the high fells a map is essential. Only two walks in this guide, the Walla Crag and Dock Tarn walks, approach being serious walks where the possession of a map is advisable. For the rest it may well be possible to get by without a map by simply relying on the directional notes and sketch maps provided. However, it is always good to have a map; I never like to be without. Three Ordnance Survey Maps are suitable:

Outdoor Leisure 4 - English Lakes North Western : Scale 1:25,500
This is an incredibly detailed map and covers all the walks described in this guide. There is one slight drawback to these maps however - see the caption on page 33

The 'One Inch' Tourist Map of the Lake District. Scale 1: 63,360.
This map covers all the walks in this guide and indeed all the rest of the fells in the Lake District. One inch on the map represents a mile on the ground.

Landranger Series Sheet 89. Scale 1:50,000
This covers all the walks in this guide. Although only a slightly larger scale than the 'One Inch' map it is surprisingly clearer.

What Else to Take

The highest point reached on any of the walks in this guide is about 1,300 feet on the Dock Tarn Walk, even so given how the weather can change in the Lake District the following items will be of advantage - unless it is a really hot day: a waterproof or windproof outer jacket, sturdy boots with a good sole pattern, hat and gloves and spare warm clothing, a comfortable day sack, food and something to drink. And to be really safe if you go above 1000 feet: a compass, torch and whistle. To check on Lake District weather conditions phone 017687 75757.

Linking walks together

Whilst this guide describes fourteen separate walks altogether, five of them can be readily linked together to create a number of other walks As follows:

Keswick to Ashness Bridge

Follow the Friar's Crag and Calfclose Bay walk (pages 16 - 17) as far as directional note 4. Here strike up to the Borrowdale Road. Cross the road on to a path which leads up to Great Wood car park and follow the Dean's Trod walk (pages 20 - 21) returning by the lake shore route to the National Trust cairn where you can return to the Calfclose walk.

Keswick to High Lodore

As above until you reach Ashness Bridge then follow the Surprise View walk (pages 22 - 23) from directional note 2 onwards. Return to Keswick by bus.

Keswick to Rosthwaite

As on the Keswick to Ashness Bridge route as far as Ashness Bridge itself then follow directional notes 2 and 3 on the Surprise View walk (pages 22 - 23). To reach Watendlath Beck where you can follow the the Watendlath Valley walk (pages 30 - 31) from directional note 2 onwards. Return to Keswick by bus.

High Lodore to Stonethwaite

Follow the the Watendlath Valley walk (pages 30 - 31) till you reach the hamlet of Watendlath then follow the Dock Tarn walk (pages 32 - 33).

The second and third of these walks can be shortened by a mile and a half roughly by starting from Great Wood car park thus:-

Great Wood to High Lodore

Follow the Dean's Trod walk (pages 20 - 21) as far as Ashness Bridge then follow the Surprise View walk (pages 22 - 23) from directional note 2 onwards. Return to Great Wood by bus.

Great Wood to Rosthwaite

As above to Ashness Bridge then follow directional notes 2 and 3 on the Surprise View walk (pages 22 - 23) to reach Watendlath Beck where you can follow the the Watendlath Valley walk (pages 30 - 31) from directional note 2 onwards. Return to Great Wood by bus.

Bionn gach tosnú lag

Castlehead 529 feet

Distance	1 3/4 miles
Total Feet of Climbing	250 feet
Suggested Time	1 hour
Starting point	Moot Hall, Keswick. (NY 266 234)

For the effort involved in reaching the top of Castlehead the rewards are quite spectacular: an impressive view down the length of Derwentwater towards the tallest mountains in England. Two benches and a scenic view finder plaque on top of this miniature summit assist the visitor there to enjoy these sights in better comfort and with better awareness.

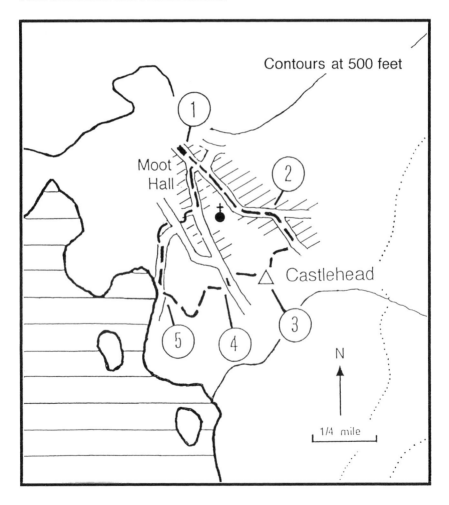

1   From the entrance of the Moot Hall leave the Market Square on the road running between the bread shop and the Keswick Lodge Hotel. Continue on past the George Hotel in to St. John's Street and on past the cinema and St. John's church. Just before the road begins pulling sharply uphill leading off to the right is a road called Springs Road. (1/2 mile)

2   Two hundred yards along Springs Road leading off to the right is a signposted, enclosed, surfaced pathway leading towards a wooded hillock - Castlehead. After passing through a kissing gate the path enters the wood surrounding Castlehead and branches in two. Follow the right hand branch. This path also branches in two at a point where it reaches the corner post of a field that projects in to the wood. Follow the left hand branch to the top of Castlehead. (1/4 mile)

3   From the summit retrace your steps. On your descent cut across to a very obvious wooden bench from which the town of Keswick can be viewed. A yard or two beyond the bench is a path which leads down to the Borrowdale road. Where it branches in two take the right hand option. On reaching the road cross straight over on to a footpath following the other side of the road. (Watch out for traffic!) (1/8 mile)

4   Follow the footpath downhill for about fifty yards to where a flight of steps leads off to the right giving access to an enclosed pathway leading to Cockshot wood. On entering the copse turn left. This path follows the boundary of the wood and eventually reaches a surfaced roadway following the shoreline of the lake. (1/2 mile)

5   Here turn right. On reaching the new theatre it becomes possible to use a walkway on the left hand side of the road rather than road itself. This walkway after a few hundred yards veers away from the road and passes beneath it by way of a subway. This brings you to a short bricked roadway. On reaching the top of this road turn left to return to the centre of Keswick. (1/2 mile)

Was there a Keswick Castle?

Despite its name there is no record or evidence of Castlehead ever having been a fortification. However, Keswick does seem to have had a castle once - or at least a fortified dwelling constructed in the early thirteenth century which was soon allowed to decay after passing to the Radcliffe family in 1317. Around 1460 the stone was seemingly used to build a house on Lord's Isle on Derwentwater. The site of this castle is unknown but it is thought to have been at Castlerigg (NY 28 22), hence the name no doubt, an area a mile east of Castlehead. In 1903 attempts were made to find some evidence of this fortification without success.

Newlands Valley

Distance	2 1/2 miles
Total Feet of Climbing	150 feet
Suggested Time	1 hour
Starting points	Gutherscale Car Park (NY 248 212)
	or
	Hawse End Landing Stage (NY 251 213) using the lake launch (see page 36) Adds an extra half a mile.

Newlands is a pastoral dale with many shapely conical peaks surrounding it. This walk is an easy saunter around the middle part of the valley which affords a good appreciation of these pleasing qualities.

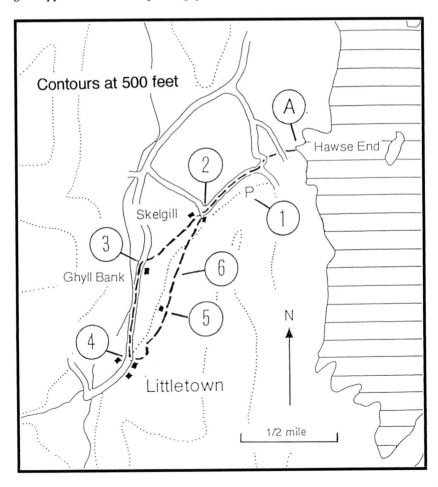

To reach Gutherscale car park by car from Keswick leave Keswick on the A66 heading westwards. Take the direction signs for Portinscale. Once in Portinscale follow signs for Grange. After crossing a cattle grid turn right on a sharp hairpin bend on to a road sign posted for Skelgill. The car park is a short distance down this road. Parking spaces are very limited but verge side parking is possible beforehand.

A To reach Gutherscale by public transport take the lake launch to Hawse End. From the landing stage a path pulls uphill to join a surfaced access road. Here turn right. Within a hundred yards or so, on the left hand side of the road, is a wooden signpost which points to a pathway for Cat Bells leading off to the left following the side of a stone wall. The path soon joins the Portinscale to Grange road. Follow the road uphill across a cattle grid. Where the road makes a sharp turn going off to the right is a narrow lane leading to Gutherscale car park (1/4 mile)

1   From the car park continue along the road in a southerly direction towards the hamlet of Skelgill. On reaching the hamlet the road turns sharp right downhill past Skelgill farm. Where it turns sharp right again leading off to the left is a trackway leading to Low Skelgill Farm. A moss covered slate sign indicates that it is also a right of way leading to Ghyll Bank. (3/8 mile)

2   The trackway passes the front of Low Skelgill to a six bar gate. Passing through the gate the right of way continues along the line of the fence to your right through two gateways and then directly across the third field you enter towards a currently gateless gateway abutted with two slate posts. Passing between these posts the path crosses a rush filled paddock to a narrow gateway giving access to a roadway. (1/2 mile)

3   Here turn left. Eventually the road comes to the hamlet of Littletown. (1/2 mile)

4   Just before entering the hamlet an enclosed trackway leads off to the left which is signposted as being a public footpath to Skelgill. The trackway eventually leads, somewhat surprisingly, to an isolated dwelling: East House. (1/4 mile)

5   Passing through a five bar gate next to East House the right of way continues as a footpath directly ahead to a second five bar gate. From there on it follows a line of hawthorn bushes which sometime in the past was obviously part of a more substantial field boundary. Where this line of bushes ends progress directly ahead to a tall wooden wall stile next to which is a gate. (1/4 mile)

6   From the gate the right of way continues along a very obvious greened over trackway through three more gateways to the gable end of Skelgill Farm. Passing through a final gateway at the gable end of the farm you return back to the road on which you began. Here turn right to return back to the car park (3/4 mile) or Hawse End boat landings (1 mile).

Seatoller to Seathwaite

Distance	2 3/4 miles there and back
Total Feet of Climbing	Negligible
Suggested Time	1 hour
Starting point	Seatoller car park/ Borrowdale bus terminus (NY 244 138)

This is a fairly level walk at the far end of the Borrowdale where the valley becomes quite wild and rugged in appearance. Seathwaite holds the unenviable record of being the wettest inhabited place in England: about 120 inches of rain each year falls on it. Without much doubt it is perhaps also the most visited farmyard in England as it is the most popular starting point for walks on to the high fells of Lakeland. There are tea rooms in both hamlets.

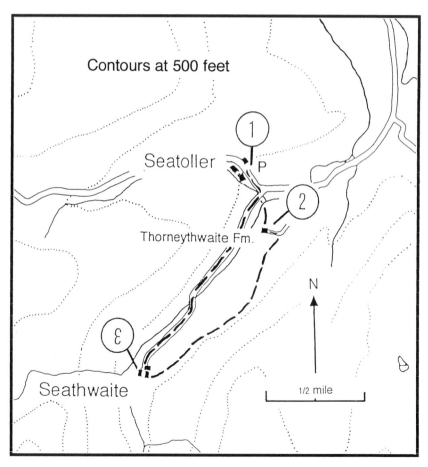

Contours at 500 feet

Seatoller

Thorneythwaite Fm.

Seathwaite

N

1/2 mile

1 From the bus terminus at the entrance of the Seatoller car park turn left to follow the Borrowdale road downhill a hundred yards and turn right on to the Seathwaite road. Within the space of a few yards on the left hand side is a six bar gate. After passing through this gate, and striding a few yards in to the field it gives access to on your right you should observe a broad footbridge spanning the River Derwent. After crossing this bridge head directly for Thornythwaite Farm straight ahead of you, using on the way a tall wall stile or the gateway next to it. (1/4 mile)

2 Leave the farm by way of the its access road. Immediately after passing through a second six bar gate turn right on to a signposted public footpath to Seathwaite which runs between a wire fence and a stone wall. The path soon crosses over a stile after which it quickly links up with a trackway. Passing through a paired five bar gate and kissing gate the quality of the trackway becomes much rougher and after passing through a second gateway reduces to the status of a simple footpath. The line of this path, however, is very obvious and is also effectively waymarked with a series of gateways all the way to the hamlet of Seathwaite. (1 1/4 mile)

3 From Seathwaite follow the road back to Seatoller. (1 1/4 mile)

What's in a Name?

The names Seathwaite and Seatoller are both Nordic in origin. The common syllable -"sea" - in each name, however, has a different root in each case. In Seathwaite's case it comes from word 'sef' meaning sedges and in Seatoller's case it comes from word 'sætr' meaning summer pasture. The second compound - thwaite - in the name Seathwaite is, of course, a very common one in Lakeland and simply means a clearing, thus - the clearing amongst the sedges. In the case of Seatoller the second compound is thought to come from the word "alor" meaning alder tree, thus - the summer pastures amongst the alders.

There are two other Seathwaites in the Lake District - one in the Duddon valley and one just outside Ambleside. At one time therefore, before the county of Cumbria was created in the early seventies, though all three Seathwaites were in the Lake District they were each in a separate county: Cumberland, Westmorland and Lancashire. The name Seatoller however is to be found only in Borrowdale.

The River Derwent

Distance	3 1/2 miles
Total Feet of Climbing	100 feet
Suggested Time	1 1/2 hours
Starting point	Seatoller car park/ Borrowdale bus terminus (NY 244 138)

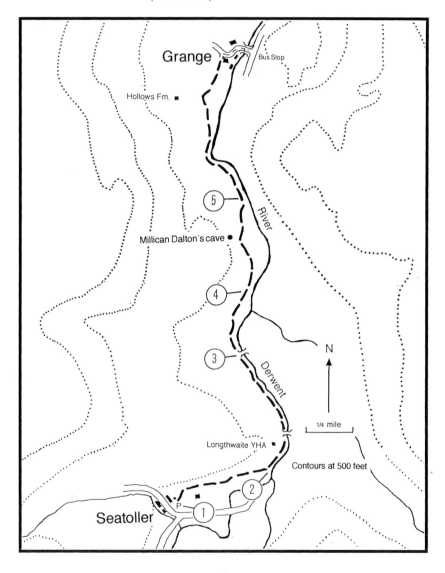

This riverside walk is made possible using the services of the Borrowdale bus (see page 36) starting from the route's terminus and returning to it in the village of Grange - a suitable place to wait for a bus as the village has two cafés.

1   Leave the rear of the car park where the Borrowdale bus terminates via a trackway waymarked with a yellow arrow which leads up to a six bar gate. After passing through the gate within a few yards branching off to the right is a narrow pathway which soon leads to a kissing gate. Passing through this kissing gate the path becomes more substantial, skirting the edge of Johnny's Wood and eventually coming to the banks of the River Derwent. (3/4 mile)

2   Here a rocky scramble of a few yards follows before coming to a gateway giving access to Longthwaite youth hostel. Follow the access road leading from the hostel. After passing through the hostel's gateway branch left off onto a trackway leading to Longthwaite Farm. The trackway soon turns in to the farm; directly ahead, however, is a kissing gate giving access to a riverside path which eventually comes to a stone bridge spanning the Derwent. (3/4 mile)

3   Leading from the bridge is a trackway which soon comes to two wooden gates. Pass through the right hand gate which has a wooden stile beside it. From this gate the trackway continues along the river bank to a further gateway which gives access to another wood. A short distance in to this wood the trackway branches in two. (1/4 mile)

4   As a small sign indicates, the left hand branch is the correct branch to follow. Wandering through some old quarry workings the track, now more of a pathway, branches in two. Take the right hand broader option. *[Or if wanting to see Millican Dalton's Cave follow the left branch - the topmost cavern would seem to be the one he lived in.]* This right hand branch almost immediately comes to a junction with another broad path. Here turn right. The path soon leads downhill to join the banks of the river. (3/4 mile)

5   Following the river's edge the track becomes increasingly broader. Passing through a campsite it eventually joins an access road leading to Hollows Farm. Here turn right to follow the access road to the village of Grange. Once meeting the public road turn right through the village and over Grange bridge to join the Borrowdale road where a bus stop for the Keswick bus is located. (1 mile)

Millican Dalton

Millican Dalton (1867-1947) abandoned a career in insurance to become a "Professor of Adventure" - a rock climbing guide - in the Lake District, making his home in a 'cave' on Castle Crag - in reality an abandoned quarry. Photographs of him still adorn the walls of many Lakeland hostelries, and still to be seen in his 'cave' is his carved inscription: "Don't!! Waste Words. Jump to Conclusions."

Friar's Crag and Calfclose Bay

Distance	3 1/2 miles
Total Feet of Climbing	Negligible
Suggested Time	1 1/2 hours
Starting point	Moot Hall, Keswick. (NY 266 234)

There are few residents of Keswick who will not have sauntered around this course - some do it with such such regularity one could almost set one's clock by them. Even on the bleakest of days it provides residents with a reminder of what a wonderful location they live in. It is also marked with a number of interesting memorials: two are remarked upon in the directional notes, others are left for the walker's own observations.

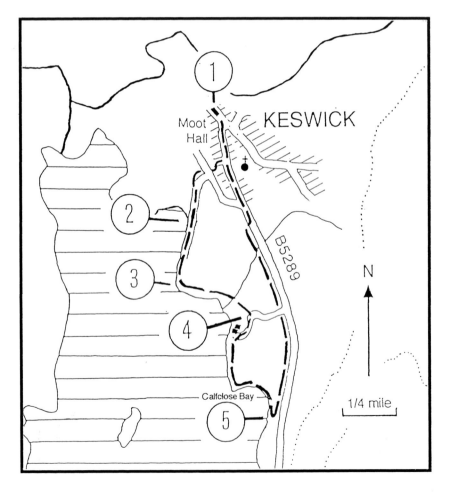

1 From the Moot Hall walk in to Lake Road - the road which runs between the Old Keswickian chip shop and Barclay's Bank. (There is no sign on this road until fifty yards along it.) You soon come to George Fisher's outdoor shop. Here turn right on to a brick surfaced roadway which is actually the continuation of Lake Road. From the end of this roadway follow a distinctive pedestrian sign to your left bearing the words "Subway to the Lake". Leading out of the subway is a broad surfaced walkway which leads to the northern end of Derwentwater. (1/2 mile)

2 On reaching the lake continue along the road which follows the shoreline. The road soon terminates but leading from this termination is a broad pathway which continues to follow the lake shore. Within 100 yards this path branches in two. Bear right. The path leads to a popular viewpoint called Friar's Crag on which a bench is situated. (3/8 mile)

3 Retrace your steps for 25 yards, where a small path branches off to the right through a young copse of conifers. (In the midst of these trees looking to your left you should see a memorial to John Ruskin.) The path soon joins a broader path. Here turn right. Passing through a small gate the path leads round the edge of the lake and then enters a small wood by way of another gate. Emerging from the wood the path joins an access road leading to Stable Hills Cottage. (1/2 mile)

4 Turn right to follow this access road. Just before reaching Stable Hills Cottage a National Trust sign indicates a footpath leading off to the left following the lake shore. The path soon comes to a small copse which occupies a short headland. Emerging from this copse on the ground to the right of the path is located a memorial plaque and in line with it in the lake's margin is an unusual sculpture. From the plaque the path continues to follow the water's edge around Calfclose Bay. About three hundred yards from the plaque the path comes to a mortared cairn of stones which contains a National Trust collection box. (3/4 mile)

5 At this point the path branches in two. Follow the left hand branch which curves back towards Keswick parallelling the Borrowdale Road - the B5289. The path passes two large public notices warning against riding a horse on this path. At the second of these signs it is necessary to cross the road to join a pathway on the other side. Keep to this pathway which leads past St. John's churchyard and then directly back to the centre of Keswick. (1 1/2 miles)

St. Herbert's Island

The most isolated island one can see from Friar's Crag, almost in the middle of the lake, is called St. Herbert's Island in consequence of it being the place where the hermit monk St. Herbert once lived over thirteen centuries ago. He died in 687. Friar's Crag is said to have been the departing point for pilgrims visiting the island.

Cat Bells Terrace and
the Brandelhow Shoreline

Distance	2 1/2 miles
Total Feet of Climbing	400 feet
Suggested Time	1 1/2 hour
Starting points	Hawes End Landing Stage (NY 251 213)
	using the lake launch from Keswick see page 36
	or
	Gutherscale Car Park (NY 248 212)
	directional notes for car users in italics.

The Cat Bells terrace affords some magnificent, elevated views over Derwentwater and beyond to the Borrowdale valley - astonishing returns when compared to the effort needed to acquire them. The walk's wooded lakeshore return is one of the most attractive lakeshore paths in Lakeland. A highly pleasurable ramble for walkers of all ages and abilities.

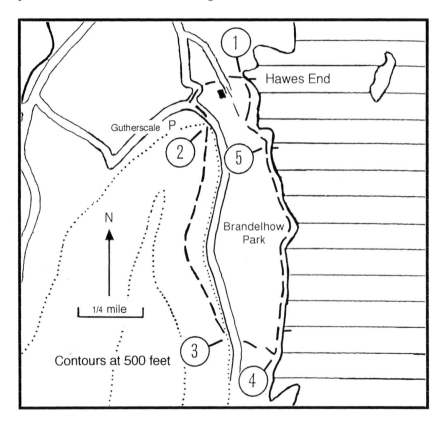

To reach Gutherscale car park by car from Keswick leave Keswick on the A66 heading westwards. Take the direction signs for Portinscale. Once in Portinscale follow signs for Grange. After crossing a cattle grid turn right on a sharp hairpin bend on to a road sign posted for Skelgill. The car park is a short distance down this road. Parking spaces are very limited but verge side parking is possible beforehand.

A *From Gutherscale car park return to the Portinscale to Grange road and turn right. In about a hundred yards leading off to the right is a signposted bridleway. (1/8 mile)*

1   From the Hawes End landing stage a path pulls uphill to join a surfaced access road. Here turn right. Within a hundred yards or so, on the left hand side of the road, is a wooden signpost which points to a pathway for Cat Bells leading off to the left following the side of a stone wall. The path soon joins the Portinscale to Grange road. Follow the road uphill across a cattle grid and round a sharp hairpin bend. About a hundred yards from this bend leading off to the right is a signposted bridleway. (1/4 mile)

2   The bridleway contours the lower slopes of the Cat Bells ridge and eventually merges back with the Portinscale to Grange road. (1 mile)

3   At this point on the other side of the road is a flight of stone steps giving access to a pathway which descends to the shoreline of Derwentwater. Just before reaching the lakeshore the path crosses a trackway and then within the space of a yard or so joins a second trackway at a point where it branches in two. Follow the right hand lower branch which leads to a narrow gate giving access to Brandelhow Wood. (Picnic tables located at this point.) (1/8 mile)

4   From the gate a path follows the shoreline of the lake finally coming to a six bar gate next to which is a kissing gate. Passing through these gates the path branches in two. (3/4 mile)

*To return to the car park follow directional note **B**. Otherwise.....*

5   Here turn left. Passing through a second gateway the path broadens in to a trackway. About a hundred yards from the second gate a small pathway branches off to the right towards the lake shore and directly back to the Hawes End landing stage. (1/4 mile)

B *Here turn left. Passing through a second gateway the path broadens to a trackway which continues through a metal gateway and then pulls slightly uphill to the access road leading to Hawes End Cottage. Here turn right. Within a hundred yards or so, on the left hand side of the road, is a wooden sign post which points to a pathway for Cat Bells leading off to the left following the side of a stone wall. The path soon joins the Portinscale to Grange road. Follow the roadway uphill back to the car park. (1/2 mile)*

Dean's Trod to Ashness Bridge

Distance	2 miles
Total Feet of Climbing	300 feet
Suggested Time	1 hour
Starting point	Great Wood car park (NY 271 213)

In the early seventies it was mooted that the Watendlath road might be closed to traffic. Preparatory to this eventuality occurring the National Trust thought it best to lay down a path to the Watendlath road from the nearest car park sited in Great Wood: thus was constructed one of the best low level paths in Lake District as regards to the views obtainable from it. The Trust's then warden for Borrowdale, Alan Dean, was very instrumental in this undertaking, a fact worthy of record and hence the name of this walk. The path leads directly to Ashness Bridge: after Tower Bridge, probably the most photographed bridge in England due to its scenic setting.

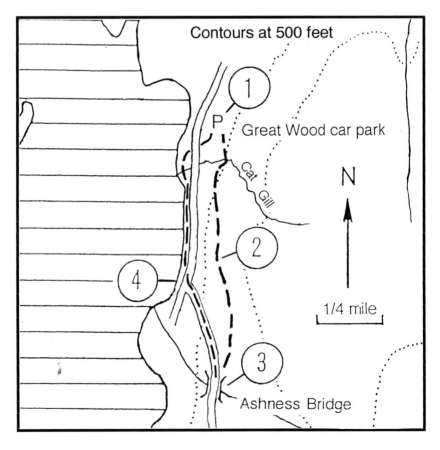

The first bus stop out of Keswick on the Borrowdale road is located at the starting point of this walk (just a few yards up from the bus stop). As it is only a mile and a half from Keswick, however, it might be preferred to walk this distance by following the Calf Close Bay Walk on page 16 as far as directional note 4.

1   Leave Great Wood car park via the stile or gate just to the right of the ticket machine. This gives access to a trackway which soon comes to a junction with another trackway. Here turn right following the line of a wire fence. Eventually the track branches into two pathways. Take the right hand branch leading to a wooden footbridge crossing Cat Gill. Once across the footbridge the path dips a little downhill and then veers off to the left, eventually coming to a large cairn sited on a natural ledge (a good place for a picnic). Here the path branches in two. (1/2 mile)

2   As a square direction sign next to the cairn indicates the left hand, higher, branch leads to Ashness Bridge. This left hand path climbs very steadily until it reaches a small gateway dedicated to Roger G. W. Frend. Passing through this gate the path descends down to the Watendlath Road and Ashness Bridge. (1/2 mile)

3   On reaching the roadway turn right and follow the road downhill to its junction with the main Borrowdale road. (1/4 mile)

4   On reaching the Borrowdale road turn right. After a distance of one mile on the right hand side of the road is the exit road out of Great Wood car park which you can use to get back to your starting point. (1 mile)

     or

     Alternatively you can try following the lake shore. This is a fairly rugged route until you come to that part of the shoreline which juts out a little into the lake. Here a more defined pathway is to be found which crosses a footbridge spanning the final section of Cat Gill and then continues through a stand of tall pine trees. Slightly more than a quarter of a mile from the footbridge the path branches in two at which point is located a mortared cairn containing a collection box for the N.T. Up to your right at this point is a gap in the wall bordering the main road. Directly opposite this gap is another gap in the wall on the other side of the road from which a path leads directly back to the car park. (1 mile)

Vivian Fisher

Wainwright's reference to the winter absence of *'Vivian Fisher, and his gate!'* from *'the popular heights above Derwentwater'* on the final page of his third volume must puzzle many readers - what was he referring to? The answer is thus: the road to Ashness bridge was once gated and Vivian Fisher, an amiable Keswickian, gained a small, harmless livelihood in summer months as a self appointed gate opener - cadging odd tips from the motorists he thus assisted.

Surprise View

Distance	2 miles
Total Feet of Climbing	600 feet
Suggested Time	1 1/2 hour
Starting point	Watendlath road end car park (NY 269 203)

Surprise View, a precipitous viewpoint overlooking Derwentwater, is one of the best known viewpoints in Lakeland. This walk employs the use of public transport both as a way of reaching the starting point and returning from the end point - alternatively one can walk all the way out from Keswick by following the first part of two other walks (see page 7) and using public transport only for the return. Located at the walk's conclusion are two very fine places of sustenance; which are more fully described at the end of the direction notes.

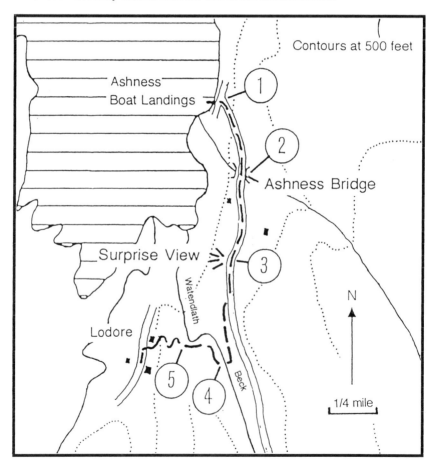

There are two ways of reaching the start of this walk using public transport: either by bus or by launch. Both have drop off points where the Watendlath road joins the Borrowdale road. Ask for the Ashness boat landings on either form of transportation.

1 From Ashness boat landing or the Watendlath road end car park follow the Watendlath road uphill to Ashness Bridge. (1/2 mile)

2 From Ashness Bridge continue on the road steeply uphill to Ashness Cottage where it runs fairly level for about a hundred yards and then pulls uphill again. At the top of this second pull, soon after the road becomes wooded on both sides, on the left had side of the road is located a mortared cairn containing a collection box for the National Trust. Opposite the cairn is the precipitous viewpoint known as Surprise View. (1/2 mile)

3 Continue along the road. In the space of another three hundred yards or so on the right hand side of the road, opposite a passing place sign, is the start of a trackway. After a distance of 500 yards the trackway comes to a six bar gate with a smaller gate next to it. Passing through the narrower gate turn right. You soon come to a bridge spanning Watendlath Beck. (1/2 mile)

4 On the other side of the bridge the path branches in two. Take the right hand branch which a triangular slate direction sign embedded in the ground indicates as leading to Lodore. The path soon passes through a kissing gate and into a wooded glade. Shortly after the path begins to descend it branches in two. Follow the left hand branch which soon comes to a wire fence spanned by a wooden stile. Once over the fence turn left. For a short distance the path follows the course of Watendlath Beck, but where the beck turns northwards the path continues directly ahead to the top of a shallow ridge. (1/4 mile)

5 From the top of this ridge the path descends to High Lodore Farm. The original path was carefully zig-zagged and with some care one can still follow the line of this path which makes the descent much easier - begin looking to your right for the first "zig" after entering a belt of birch trees. On reaching the Borrowdale Road turn left. The bus stop for the Keswick bus stands opposite the Borrowdale Hotel. (1/4 mile)

Situated in the barn of High Lodore farm is perhaps the best value for money cafe in the Lake District though seating arrangements are somewhat spartan. Plusher seating is to be had in the Borrowdale Hotel, together with a stronger type of beverage should that be your wont.

Borrowdale Terrace

1 pt. mugs of tea & great cakes!

Distance	3 1/4 miles
Total Feet of Climbing	500 feet
Suggested Time	1 1/2 hours
Starting point	Rosthwaite village shop (NY 258 149)

Borrowdale has been called the most attractive valley in the Lake District. The valley's beauty can be appreciated fully on this elevated, circular walk. Part of the walk includes a section of the old toll road over Honister Pass which was built by the quarry company which formerly operated there. In the nineteen thirties the county council wished to make this toll road public. The company, however, sought a payment of two thousand pounds to concede their rights which the council refused to pay: they constructed their own road instead. Consequently the toll road fell into disuse. This has left the humble foot wanderer the main beneficiary, for the old toll road takes by far the better line of ascent.

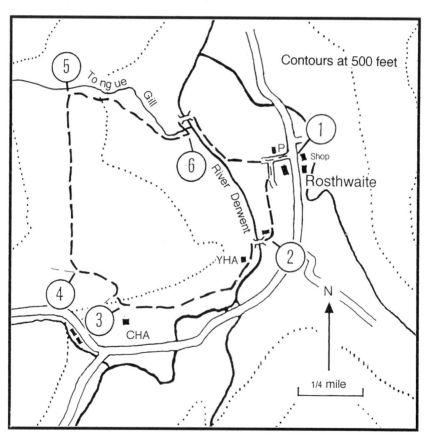

Rosthwaite car park is located a few yards down the lane opposite the village shop. The bus stop for the village is located just a few yards before the shop.

1   Walk down the narrow lane opposite the village shop past the village hall and on reaching Yew Tree Farm turn left through the village of Rosthwaite till you reach a large corrugated iron shed belonging to Clare's cottage on your right. Here turn right on to an enclosed trackway running besides the shed. Twenty yards along this trackway on the left hand is a six bar gate from which proceeds a public footpath. The path passes through three small fields via a stile and gateway to a compact group of small white cottages where it joins a narrow roadway. (3/8 mile)

2   Here turn right. Follow the road over a stone bridge to Longthwaite Youth Hostel. From the front of the hostel a broad path continues southwards to the river's edge where it becomes quite rocky to such a degree a chain has been affixed to the rocks to assist the walker's passage. After this awkward section the path leads away from the river along the edge of Johnny's Wood. As the path approaches a large wooden building - the Countrywide Holiday's Glaramara House - it curves right up to a kissing gate. (3/4 mile)

3   After passing through this kissing gate bear left but only for 10 yards or so where leading uphill to the right is a thin green path leading through some holly trees. Reaching a beck you also come to a trackway. Cross both and continue uphill towards some tall conifer trees some hundred feet higher up. Coming level with these trees you reach a broad trackway - the old toll road leading to Honister Quarry. Follow this old road uphill. 150 yards after the second five bar gate you pass through, and about thirty yards before the next, on the right side of the track is a small yellow arrow waymark. (1/4 mile)

4   The waymark indicates a pathway pulling uphill to a narrow gateway sited in a stone wall a hundred feet up the fellside. After passing through this gate turn right to follow the path initially following the side of the wall you have just passed through. The path crosses two footbridges. A couple of hundred yards from the second bridge a trackway cuts across the pathway - an isolated hawthorn bush marks the junction. (3/4 mile)

5   Here turn right and follow this distinct trackway which soon passes through a substantial wooden six bar gate downhill. At the foot of descent head for a very obvious wooden footbridge by means of a small stile set in a small section of wooden fencing next to Tongue Gill. From the footbridge follow the banks of Tongue Gill to its confluence with the River Derwent. (1/2 mile)

6   Here turn left to cross a footbridge which spans Tongue Gill in order to follow the course of the River Derwent the space of thirty odd yards to a substantial stone bridge which spans the River Derwent. From this bridge a broad trackway leads back to Rosthwaite village. (1/2 mile)

Twixt 3.30 and 5 o'clock probably the best tea and scones in Lakeland are served in the Royal Oak Hotel in the centre of Rosthwaite.

Stonethwaite Valley

Distance	4 1/2 miles
	(can be shortened 2 1/4 miles see directional note 2)
Total Feet of Climbing	Negligible
Suggested Time	2 hours
Starting point	Rosthwaite (NY 258 149)

This is an easy wander round the south eastern arm of the Borrowdale valley with a glimpse of the wild emptiness of the Langstrath valley. Some impressive crags overlook the valley: Eagle Crag is especially striking. The settlement of Stonethwaite, pleasing as it looks, may well be the least sunny settlement in England. For three months, from mid-November to mid-February, no ray of sun can reach it. During that period should there be a cloudless day poor Stonethwaite stands in the shadow of its surrounding fells due to the sun then not being high enough in the firmament.

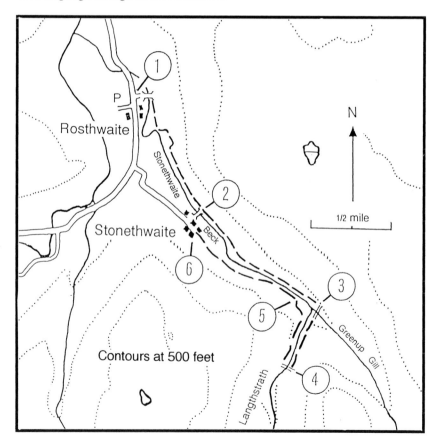

Rosthwaite car park is located a few yards down the lane opposite the village shop. The bus stop for the village is located a few yards north of the shop.

1   From the bus stop in Rosthwaite after a few strides southwards turn left on to an access road leading to Hazel Bank. Immediately after crossing a stone bridge turn sharp right on to a stony bridleway following the course of Stonethwaite Beck and signposted as leading to Stonethwaite. Eventually the bridleway comes to a five bar gate just before which branching off to the right is a trackway leading over a stone bridge to Stonethwaite. (1 mile)

2   Unless you wish to foreshorten the walk by turning right into the hamlet of Stonethwaite continue forward through the five bar gate. A wooden signpost close by indicates the bridleway leads to Grasmere. Eventually the path draws level with the mouth of the Langstrath valley where Langstrath Beck and Greenup Gill merge to form Stonethwaite Beck. Shortly beyond this confluence in the wall to your right is located a gate giving access to broad footbridge spanning Greenup Gill. (1 mile)

3   From the footbridge a path continues uphill following the course of Langstrath Beck, sections of which have been cobbled due to the boggy nature of the ground. Eventually the path comes to another broad footbridge this time spanning Langstrath Beck. (1/4 mile)

4   Crossing this bridge brings you to a much broader pathway. Here turn right. Some six hundred yards along this pathway, a few paces beyond a smooth isolated boulder which stands beside it, leading off to the right, initially cobbled, is a narrower pathway leading to a wooden stile sited close to the edge of Stonethwaite Beck. (3/8 mile)

5   From the stile the path continues along the banks of Stonethwaite Beck across a second ladder type stile and on through Stonethwaite campsite. The right of way continues from the camp site through a wooden gate and across the field you enter to a second ·gateway where it becomes a trackway. The trackway crosses the next two fields to the hamlet of Stonethwaite where it joins a surfaced roadway. (3/4 mile)

6   Continue on the roadway through the village to the main Borrowdale road. Here turn right to return back to Rosthwaite. (1 mile)

Both Stonethwaite and Rosthwaite have hotels which have public bars, respectively - the Langstrath Hotel and the Scafell Hotel. Both villages also have tea rooms.

Castlerigg Stone Circle

Distance	4 1/2 miles
Total Feet of Climbing	450 feet
Suggested Time	2 hours
Starting point	Moot Hall, Keswick. (NY 266 234)

After Stonehenge Castlerigg Stone Circle is probably the best known stone circle in England. It raises many questions: What was it for? How was it built? Why is it positioned where it is? Certainly it is sited on a very panoramic view point: Helvellyn, Cat Bells, Causey Pike, Grisedale Pike, Skiddaw and Blencathra can all be seen. Castle Lane, running past the circle, makes for a particularly wonderful summer's evening saunter if the day is fine. The walk is particularly suitable for anyone newly arrived in Keswick with only a few hours of daylight left to them in which to discover their suroundings.

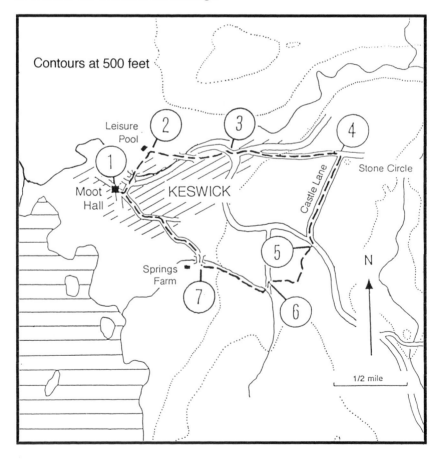

1   From the entrance of the Moot Hall leave the Market Square on the road running between the bread shop and the Keswick Lodge Hotel. Turn left at the corner of the hotel into Station Street which continues as Station Road after crossing an intersection with the main road through Keswick. Station Road leads directly to Keswick's Leisure Pool. (1/4 mile)

2   Walk round the right hand side of the pool: you soon see to your right Keswick's old railway station. Follow the old railway line, now a footpath, running in front of it. Five hundred yards after crossing the river Greta the line passes under a bridge. Immediately after passing under this bridge to your left is a flight of steps leading up to the road which crosses over this bridge. (1/2 mile)

3   On reaching the road turn left. The road soon branches in two. Take the left hand branch for about fifty yards and then branch right on to a country lane signposted as leading to the Stone Circle. This is a steepish pull. On reaching the brow of the climb a narrow lane, called Castle Lane, leads off to the right. The stone circle is situated in the field bounded by these two roads. (1 mile)

4   Follow Castle Lane to its junction with the main Keswick to Windermere road - the A591. (3/4 mile)

5   Directly across the road is a paired five bar gate and kissing gate next to which is a metal signpost indicating that the trackway leading from these gates leads to Walla Crag. The right of way follows the right hand edge of the first three fields you enter. At the end of the third the route takes a sharp right hand turn and follows a sunken trackway that eventually comes to another country lane. (1/2 mile)

(At this point a few hundred yards to the right is situated The Heights Hotel, the garden of which in summer months is perhaps the finest place in northern Lakeland in which to enjoy sustenance whilst watching the sun descend and listening to an avian chorus. But this is a digression, very pleasant as it is, to follow the actual walk from the point at which you join the road....)

6   Here turn left. Within the space of fifteen yards branch right down to a kissing gate. A signpost next to the gate indicates that the path leading from it leads back to Keswick. It does so by firstly crossing a stream, called Brockle Beck, by way of a narrow foot bridge, and then turning right to follow the course of Brockle Beck to Springs Farm. (1/2 mile)

7   Follow the road leading from Springs Farm to its junction with the Ambleside road. Here turn left. The road leads directly back to the centre of Keswick. (3/4mile)

The Watendlath Valley

Distance	3 1/2 miles
Total Feet of Climbing	900 feet
Suggested Time	2 hours
Starting point	High Lodore (NY 262 183)

Coming upon the Watendlath valley is a revelation - certainly the way this route approaches it. This walk then should seem like a walk of discovery. At the head of the valley is situated a settlement idyllic enough to stir the Muse of a poet - well, a novelist at least: this is the setting of Hugh Walpole's *Herries Chronicles*. The descent to Rosthwaite affords one of the most glorious views in Lakeland - the head of Borrowdale and the highest hills in Cumbria. The Borrowdale bus (see page 36) provides transport both to the walk's starting point and back from its conclusion in Rosthwaite.

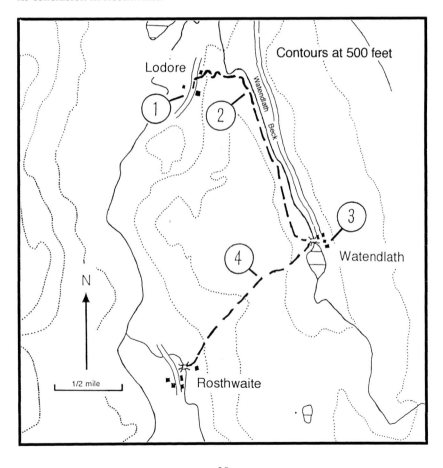

1 From the Borrowdale Hotel walk uphill along the road for fifty yards or so and turn right through a gate partially made of cast iron wheels in to High Lodore farm. Follow the trackway leading round the back of the farm where leading off to the right from the trackway is the start of a very distinct footpath. The path climbs steeply uphill and eventually reaches a gap in a stone wall. Passing through this gap the path dips down slightly to follow the dramatic course of Watendlath Beck and soon comes to a wooden stile spanning a wire fence. Cross over this stile and follow the path leading from it. The path veers right from the river through a narrow cutting in the crags and soon comes to a kissing gate. Here the path turns sharp left back towards the river and a wooden footbridge spanning across it. (1/2 mile)

2 A few yards before the footbridge on the ground is a unique triangular direction plaque. As the plaque indicates by taking the path leading off to the right, following the course of the river, you eventually reach the hamlet of Watendlath, gaining access to the hamlet by crossing a small packhorse bridge which spans the river named after it. (1 1/4 miles)

3 Return to the packhorse bridge and turn left. The route soon passes through a gate after which it branches in two. As a nearby wooden signpost indicates the right hand branch leads to Rosthwaite. The path climbs 300 feet to the top of a modest pass between the valleys of Watendlath and Borrowdale. (1/2 mile)

4 The descent to Rosthwaite is one of clearest routes in Lakeland and has really only one possible point of confusion: near the end of the descent when the path comes to a six bar gate. Be sure to pass through this gate rather than continuing on the path which progresses straight ahead to Stonethwaite. Eventually the bridleway reaches a surfaced access road. Follow the access road over a stone bridge to the main Borrowdale road. The bus stop for the bus back to Keswick is on the opposite side of the road just to your left. (1 mile)

The Lost Inn

Some centuries ago the packhorse was the main means by which goods were transported through the Lake District. During that period the main route to Rosthwaite and upper Borrowdale was actually via Watendlath as there was then no main road following the River Derwent. This is the reason, no doubt, why Watendlath once had an inn. Nothing remains of this inn today, unfortunately, but a large corner foundation stone just to the left of the hamlet's packhorse bridge.

Dock Tarn

Starting point	Watendlath	High Lodore
Grid Reference	(NY 275 163)	(NY 262 183)
Distance	3 miles	5 miles
Total Feet of Climbing	450 feet	1100 feet
Suggested Time	2 hours	3 hours

This walk is a more adventurous conclusion to the Watendlath walk described on the previous two pages - though it can be done as described using public transport (see page 36). It is, however, not an easy ramble but a true fell walk. You therefore need to be well shod - the descent is particularly steep and rocky. The views on this descent, however, are spectacular. If begun from High Lodore, especially, this is one of the most exciting short walks in Lakeland.

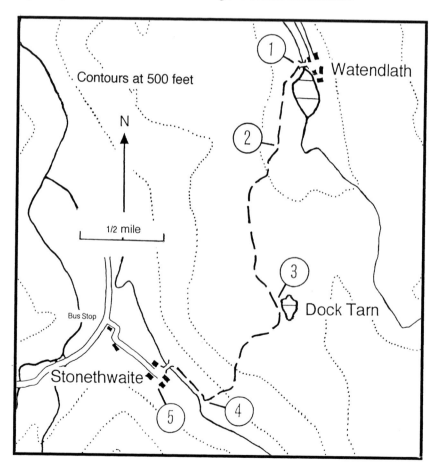

1   Cross over the packhorse bridge spanning the outflow of Watendlath Tarn and turn left. The trackway soon comes to a five bar gate and kissing gate after which it branches in two. A signpost at this point indicates that the left hand branch leads to Dock Tarn. This route soon becomes enclosed and eventually the track comes to a five bar gate next to which is a stone stile. (1/2 mile)

2   Here the trackway becomes more rugged, less defined and unenclosed. After a hundred yards or so it crosses a small beck. Here, as a waymark arrow indicates, the right of way branches off to the right initially following the course of the beck. The path soon comes to another five bar gate and kissing gate beyond which is a small sign requesting the walker to bear left. A short distance beyond this sign is yet another sign where the path branches in two. As this sign indicates the left hand branch leads to Dock Tarn. Although from here on there are sections of the path which are very boggy or very rugged the line of the path is always obvious. After passing through a kissing gate there follows a steep but mostly cobbled ascent to Dock Tarn. (1 mile)

3   The path continues along the western side of the tarn. A hundred yards past the end of tarn the path begins descending to Stonethwaite at which point some remarkable views begin developing. The descent takes a winding course and it is frequently unclear where it might lead. However, the path is so distinct there is no possibility of losing the line of it or taking another route by mistake for none exists. The descent becomes particularly steep after passing the ruin of a stone hut and entering an area of woodland. It is, however, also cobbled. Emerging from the wood the path eventually reaches a trackway following the line of a long stone wall. (3/4 mile)

4   Here turn right. After passing through a five bar gate turn left onto a trackway which crosses a bridge spanning Stonethwaite Beck into the hamlet of Stonethwaite. (1/4 mile)

5   Here is joined a surfaced roadway. Turn right and follow the road to its junction with the main Borrowdale road. Directly on the opposite side of the road is the bus stop for Keswick. (1/2 mile)

Walking on Water!

As marvellous as the Ordnance Survey maps undoubtedly are they can sometimes cause confusion due to rights of way being represented where no footpath actually exists. Nowhere has this been more evident than on maps representing Dock Tarn where, certainly up to 1998, a right of way has been shown as passing through the southern end of the tarn! A right of way has certainly existed here but no footpath ever has. In 1998 an application was made to have this right of way discontinued! The path actually used in this area hitherto has been marked with a black, dashed line.

Walla Crag 1234 feet

Distance	5 3/4 miles
Total Feet of Climbing	1000 feet
Suggested Time	3 hours
Starting point	Moot Hall, Keswick. (NY 266 234)

Walla Crag provides an excellent view over Keswick and Derwentwater whilst the view on the descent from the summit towards Ashness is one of the finest prospects in England.

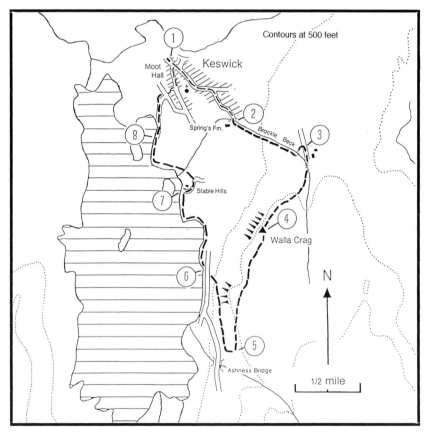

1 From the entrance of the Moot Hall leave the Market Square on the road running between the bread shop and the Keswick Lodge Hotel. Continue past the George Hotel on to St John's Street and past St John's church. Just before the road begins to pull uphill turn right into Springs Road which leads to Springs farm where the road terminates. (3/4 mile)

2   Bear left past the farm's stable block and through a five bar gate on to a pathway which follows the course of Brockle Beck.   The pathway soon branches in two. Follow the right hand branch signposted as leading to Walla Crag. This branch continues to follow the course of Brockle Beck until it eventually crosses the beck by way of a narrow footbridge after which it climbs up to a kissing gate which gives access to another roadway. (1/2 mile)

3   Here turn right. The road soon branches in two. Take the right hand branch. The road soon terminates where another footbridge crosses Brockle Beck. Beginning from the other side of the footbridge is a signposted path to Walla Crag. This route soon branches in two. Take the right hand, more trodden, route which after a climb of 300 odd feet comes to a kissing gate sited in a short section of wire fence from which a path leads along the edge of Walla Crag to its highest point. (3/4 mile)

4   From the summit the path continues along the edge of the crag back to the crag's enclosing wall where a wooden stile is located. On the other side of this stile the path branches in two. Take the left hand branch. After a few hundred yards this path also branches in two. Take the right hand branch which descends towards Ashness. After roughly half a mile this path branches in two - though you may easily not notice this. The right hand branch heads directly towards a small road bridge, Ashness Bridge, whilst the left hand seemingly heads towards Ashness Farm. The left hand branch is the most distinctive of the two which is fortuitous as this is the better to follow. It leads to a tall ladder stile spanning a stone wall. (1 mile)

5   Do not cross the stile but follow the line of the wall it crosses downhill. This soon brings you to a narrow gateway in the wall where two other paths converge. Here turn right and take the lower of these two paths. After passing under Falcon Crag follow a narrower path branching off to the left down to the Borrowdale road the B 5289. (3/4 mile)

6   On the other side of the road is a walkway. Follow this walkway for twenty yards or so to a break in the embankment which comes to bound this side of the road from which a steep path zig-zags down to the lake shore where a shoreline path is located. This lake shore path eventually brings you to a group of buildings called Stable Hills. (3/4 mile)

7   Here the right of way continues along the access lane leading to Stable Hills. 150 yards along this lane, on the left hand side, is located a dual gateway giving access to a path leading through a small stretch of woodland. Emerging from this copse the path continues as a lake shore path which eventually comes to the terminus of a surfaced roadway. (5/8 mile)

8   Continue along this roadway. On reaching Keswick's new theatre it becomes possible to use a walkway on the left hand side of the road. This walkway soon veers away from the road and then passes beneath it by way of a subway giving access to a short bricked roadway. At the top of this road turn left to return to the centre of Keswick. (5/8 mile)

Public Transport

The start of all the walks in this guide, where they do not start in Keswick itself, are reachable from Keswick using public transport. In a number of walks public transport is used as a way of returning to the starting point. The services which make this possible are as follows:

The Borrowdale Bus - Service 79

This runs from Keswick bus station (opposite the Lakes supermarket on Tithebarn Street) to Seatoller along the B5289. It runs roughly hourly all year round except Sundays in the winter. During the summer school holidays it runs half hourly. The service is operated by Cumberland Motors, telephone 0870 608 2 608. Bus timetables are usually well displayed at all bus stops.

Keswick Launch

The Keswick and Derwentwater Launch Company operates a launch service around Derwentwater calling at various point around the lake including Hawes End and Ashness. Operates all year round with greater frequency, of course, in the summer. For telephone enquiries phone 017687 72263.

The Watendlath Wanderer

A minibus service from Keswick to Watendlath is operated by the National Trust on Sundays only from Easter to October - seven trips a day. The minibus picks up at the National Trust's Lakeside Information Centre near the new theatre. For telephone enquiries phone 017687 73780. The service is free!

Copies of timetables for all the above services are available from the Tourist Information Centre in the Moot Hall in the centre of Keswick, telephone 017687 72645.

August 2000